PEACE AND THE LIMITS OF WAR

Transcending the Classical Conception of Jihad

LOUAY M. SAFI

THE INTERNATIONAL INSTITUTE OF ISLAMIC THOUGHT
LONDON · WASHINGTON

SECOND EDITION, 2003 CE
FIRST EDITION, 2001 CE

THE INTERNATIONAL INSTITUTE OF ISLAMIC THOUGHT
P.O. BOX 669, HERNDON, VA 22070, USA

LONDON OFFICE
P.O. BOX 126, RICHMOND, SURREY TW9 2UD, UK

ISBN 1–56564–402–6 *paperback*

Typeset by Sohail Nakhooda
Cover Design by Saddiq Ali
Printed in the United Kingdom
by Biddles Limited, Guildford and King's Lynn
www.biddles.co.uk

PERSPECTIVES ON ISLAMIC THOUGHT SERIES

Contents

Foreword

THE INTERNATIONAL INSTITUTE OF ISLAMIC THOUGHT (IIIT) has great pleasure in presenting a newly revised and edited edition of Dr. Louay Safi's treatise *Peace and the Limits of War: Transcending the Classical Conception of Jihad*, published under its Perspectives on Islamic Thought Series. Since publication of the first edition in 2001, the work has received wide attention from a growing circle of readership, generating enough interest, felt the publishers, to warrant the production of a second edition.

Peace and the concept of jihad are issues of vital importance. Firmly on the agenda of worldwide political debate and discourse they frame much of the parameters of analysis on Islam and the Middle East today. This work is an important addition to this analysis. Through careful and meticulous study into an area fraught with cultural misconceptions and near total confusion the author has sought to elucidate some of the subjective and negative fundamentals which have come to dominate much of the discourse on the issue today and restore a balanced understanding.

We would like to express our thanks to Dr. Louay M. Safi, who, throughout the various stages of the production of this edition, cooperated with the editorial group at the IIIT London Office.

We would also like to thank the editorial and production team at the London Office and those who were involved in the completion of this book: Sylvia Hunt, Sohail Nakhooda, Kereema Altomare, Shiraz Khan and Dr. Maryam Mahmood, all of whom worked tirelessly in preparing the book for publication. May God reward them and the author for all their efforts.

Jumada II 1424 IIIT LONDON OFFICE
August 2003

Author's Preface to the First Edition

THIS MONOGRAPH is an expanded version of an article published in the *American Journal of Islamic Social Sciences (AJISS)* in 1988, under the title "War and Peace in Islam." The article attempted then to clarify some of the misconceptions surrounding the notion of jihad. Thirteen years later, the same misconceptions and misunderstandings regarding war and peace in Islam are wide-spread in both the Muslim societies and the West.

The attacks on the United States on September 11, 2001, by an apparently religiously inspired group, brought to the fore the question of jihad and war, and led a few misinformed and misguided individuals to confuse the Islamic concept of jihad with the medieval concept of holy war. The equation of the two is erroneous and misleading. Holy wars were fought in medieval Europe in the name of God against infidels, because the latter were perceived to stand against God. Jihad, on the other hand, is fought to repel aggression and lift the oppression of a brutal force, and is never directed at the other's faith. The fact that both are based on religious motivation does not make them equal. Religious motives have historically inspired both the noblest and the basest actions.

I, therefore, do hope that this monograph will contribute to bringing more meaningful discussion of the notion of jihad and the conception of war and peace in Islamic tradition. I also hope to be able to illustrate that the Islamic worldview and values stand on the side of world peace and global justice, and against aggression and brutality.

I wish to thank two good friends who have encouraged me to refine the early article I wrote on peace and war into the current monograph, Jamal Barzinji and Sayyid M. Syeed. Their encouragement and support are greatly appreciated.

INTRODUCTION

ISLAM IS A RELIGION OF PEACE. This fact is borne out by both Islamic teachings and the very name of "Islam." The term Islam essentially means to submit and surrender one's will to a higher truth and a transcendental law, so that one can lead a meaningful life informed by the divine purpose of creation – a life in which the dignity and freedom of all human beings can be equally protected. Islamic teachings assert the basic freedom and equality of all peoples. They stress the importance of mutual help and respect, and direct Muslims to extend friendship and goodwill to all, regardless of their religious, ethnic, or racial background.

Islam, on the other hand, permits its followers to resort to armed struggle to repel military aggression, and indeed urges them to fight oppression, brutality, and injustice. The Qur'anic term for such a struggle is jihad. Yet for many in the West, jihad is nothing less than a holy war, i.e., a war to enforce one's religious beliefs on others. Most Muslims would reject the equation of jihad with holy war, and would insist that a better description that captures the essence of the Islamic concept of jihad is a just war. There are still small and vocal groups of Muslims who conceive jihad as a divine license to use violence to impose their will on anyone whom they could brand as an infidel, including fellow Muslims who may not fit their self-proclaimed categorization of right and wrong.

The confusion about the meaning of jihad and the debate over whether jihad is a "holy war" or a "just war" are of great importance for Muslims and non-Muslims alike, particularly at this juncture of human history when the world has once again rejected narrow nationalist politics and is moving rapidly to embrace the notion of global peace and the notion of a multi-cultural and multi-religious society. It is, hence, crucial to expose the confusion of those who insist that jihad is a holy war and who place doubts on Islam's ability to support global peace. The advocates of jihad as a holy war constitute today a tiny minority of intellectuals in both Muslim societies and the West. Western scholars, who accept jihad as holy war, feed on the position of radical Muslim ideologues, as well as on generalization of the particular and exceptional to the general.

Given the fact that radical interpretations of Islam have had a disproportionate influence on the way Islam's position regarding peace and war is perceived and understood, I intend to focus my discussion on rebutting the propositions of the classical doctrine of jihad, embraced by radical Muslims, and to show that these propositions were predicated on a set of legal rulings (*aḥkām sharᶜīyyah*) pertaining to specific questions which arose under particular historical circumstances, namely, the armed struggle between the Islamic state during the Abbasid era, and the various European dynasties. I hope I will be able to demonstrate in the ensuing discussion that classical jurists did not intend to develop a holistic theory with universal claims.

I further aspire to introduce a more comprehensive conception of war and peace which takes into account the Qur'anic and Prophetic statements in their totality. This new conception is then used to establish the fundamental objectives of war as well as the basic conditions of peace.

Misunderstanding the position of Islam vis-à-vis war and peace alluded to earlier is essentially a problem of textural explication. It is a problem of how a Qur'anic text is and ought to be interpreted. What rules did classical scholars use in deriving concepts and doctrines from Islamic sources, and what rules should Muslims use today? And, because the analysis must engage the classical methods, there is no escape from employing the terminology of Islamic jurisprudence, better known as *uṣūl al-fiqh*. The legalistic and textual analysis of Islamic texts is, however, joined by a historical and analytical discussion, aimed at examining the socio-political conditions surrounding the armed jihad between the early Islamic state and the various political communities that it fought.

CHAPTER ONE

CLASSICAL VIEWS AND HISTORICAL CONDITIONS

THE DOCTRINE of jihad was developed in the first three centuries of Islam, and was influenced by the political structure of the day. We argue in this chapter that the ideas and doctrines advanced by early Muslim jurists were shaped, on the one hand, by the political organization of the Islamic polity, which recognized the moral autonomy of the various religious and ethnic communities that it compromised, and on the other hand, by the imperial politics of Byzantium.

The classical doctrine of jihad, and its corollary theory of the Two Territories, are the products of their time, and should be understood as such.

CLASSICAL DOCTRINE OF JIHAD

Although the rules and principles pertaining to relations between Islamic and non-Islamic states date back to the early Madinan period, the classical doctrine of war and peace was developed by Muslim jurists (*fuqahā'*) during the Abbasid era. The tenets of the doctrine can be found either in general law corpora under headings such as jihad, peace treaties, *amān*, or in certain special studies such as *al-kharāj* (land tax), *al-siyar* (biography/ history), etc. The work of the Muslim jurists consists mainly of rules and principles concerning the initiation and prosecution of war, rules, and principles that have been predicated on a specific perception of the role and objectives of the Islamic state in respect to other states.

Classical Muslim scholars often equated the notion of jihad with that of war. This conception of jihad failed to capture the full range of its rich meaning, thereby reducing in effect the act of jihad into the act of war. While the Qur'an often uses the word jihad in reference to the act of war, it gives the term broader meaning. The term jihad was first introduced in the Makkan Qur'an – verses 29: 6, 69 and 25:52 – long before the Muslims were permitted to fight. In the Makkan period, the term jihad was used in reference to the peaceful struggle in the cause of God:

> And those who make jihad in Our [cause], We will certainly guide them to Our paths. (29:69)

> And whoever makes jihad he does so for his own soul ... (29:6)

> Therefore, listen not to the unbelievers, but make jihad against them with the utmost strenuousness, with [the Qur'an]. (25:52)

These three verses direct the Muslims to patiently persevere in the face of Quraysh persecution and oppression, and to engage in dialogue and persuasion with the aim of reaching out and expanding the truth of Islam. It follows that fighting and using military tactics is only one of several avenues through which the duty of jihad can be discharged. The methodology of jihad includes, among other things, peaceful resistance and perseverance against oppression and tyranny, if the general conditions of the moment indicate that this approach is the most effective way to achieve the objectives of the Muslim community.

The classical doctrine of war and peace is founded on three essential propositions:[1]

1. The world is divided into two territories: *dār al-Islām*, the area subject to Islamic law, and *dār al-Ḥarb*, the area not yet brought under Islamic rule. Al-Shāfiʿī adds a third territory, *dār al-ʿAhd* or the territory of covenant. His third category, however, is superfluous, for he stipulates that a non-Islamic state may enter into a peace treaty with the Islamic state only if it renders an annual tribute of *jizyah* [poll tax]. This stipulation, therefore, puts him on the same footing with the other classical writers.

2. *Dār al-Islām* is under permanent jihad obligation until *dār al-Ḥarb* is reduced to nonexistence. Jihad is, thus, the instrument of the Islamic state to propagandize Islam and expand the territory wherein Islamic law is enforced.

3. Peaceful coexistence between *dār al-Islam* and *dār al-Ḥarb* is possible only when the latter renders an annual tribute of *jizyah* to the former.

The classical doctrine of war and peace has persisted over the centuries with a few minor and sporadic alterations. The tenets of this doctrine have been handed down unchallenged, despite several grave flaws in its development and despite its violation of some essential Islamic principles.[2]

As will be argued later, this may, in part, be attributed to the political conditions existing at the time the doctrine was articulated and developed; conditions which prevailed throughout much of Muslim history.

According to the classical Muslim jurists, a permanent state of war exists between *dār al-Islam* and *dār al-Ḥarb*. War, however, is divided into two types. First, war of domination against polytheists who have two options from which to choose: either to accept Islam or fight. Second, war of reconciliation against the People of the Book who have three possibilities to face: to accept Islam and, thus, be left alone, to pay the *jizyah*, in which case they are entitled to retain their religion and enjoy Muslim protection, or to fight the Muslim army.[3] It is clear that war, according to the foregoing view, is the normal state of things, and that peaceful relations between the Islamic and non-Islamic states is contingent on the acceptance of Islam by the non-Islamic states or their payment of annual tributes to the Islamic states.

WAR OF DOMINATION

The classical position, in regard to the principles of war and peace, has been primarily predicated on three Qur'anic verses and on one hadith:

> And fight them until there is no more persecution and religion[4] is only for God. (2:193)
>
> But when the forbidden months are past, then fight and slay the polytheists whenever you find them, and seize them, beleaguer them, and lie in wait for them in every stratagem [of war], but if they repent, and establish salah and pay their zakah, then open the way to them, for God is Oft-Forgiving, Most Merciful. (9:5)
>
> Fight those who believe not in God nor the last day, nor forbid what God and His Messenger forbade, nor acknowledge the religion of Truth, [even if they are] of the "People of the Book," until they pay the *jizyah* with willing submission and feel themselves subdued. (9:29)
>
> I have been commanded to fight the people until they say: "There is no god but God." When they say that, then their lives and property are inviolable to me, except [in the case when] the [law of] Islam allows it [to take them]. They will be answerable to God.[5]

The first verse, revealed in Madinah, has been construed by some Muslim jurists and commentators as obligating Muslims to fight non-Muslims until the latter embrace Islam, in the case of the polytheists, or pay *jizyah*, in the case of the "People of the Book." In other words, the verse has been considered as a general rule (*ḥukm ʿām*)[6] which must be interpreted in association with the particular rules revealed in the verses 9:5 and 9:29. The verse has been interpreted, in practical terms, to mean that non-Muslims should either be forced to accept Islam or be dominated by the Islamic state. Yet the immediate and direct interpretation is that the Muslims should fight non-Muslims until the latter cease attacking or persecuting them.[7] The second interpretation is not only more plausible and coherent, but also the only possible explanation (*ta'wīl*) of the verse when read in its context.

> Fight in the cause of God those who fight you, but do not commit aggression, for God loves not aggressors. (2:190)

> And slay them wherever ye catch them, and turn them out from where they have turned you out; for persecution is worse than slaughter ... (2:191)
>
> But if they cease, God is Oft-Forgiving, Most Merciful. (2:192)
>
> And fight them until there is no more persecution and religion is only for God, but if they cease, let there be no hostility except to those who practice oppression. (2:193)

The verses begin by commanding Muslims to fight those who initiate war against them, emphasizing that Muslims should never be the aggressive party. The term *ʿudwān,* translated here as "aggression," is used in the Qur'an to indicate the instigation of hostility.[8] Some jurists claim that the verse, "fight in the cause of God who fight you ..." is abrogated (*mansūkh*) by the verses of *Surat al-Tawbah,* a claim rejected by other jurists and scholars, including Ibn ʿAbbās, ʿUmar ibn ʿAbd al-ʿAzīz, Mujāhid, and others, who assert that it is a firm rule (*muḥkam*).[9] Al-Ṭabarī, who also holds that the verse is not abrogated, chooses the interpretation of ʿUmar ibn ʿAbd al-ʿAziz, who construed the verse to mean: "do not fight those who do not fight you, meaning women, children, and monks."[10] Although ʿUmar limits the application of this verse only to women, children, and monks, the verse itself provides a general rule which includes those who do not fight or show hostility against Muslims. As it will be argued later, the particularization (*takhṣīṣ*) made by ʿUmar had not been induced by the statement[11] of the text (*ʿibārah al-naṣṣ*), but rather by historical and practical considerations.

The next verse, 2:191, posits the reason for which the Muslims had been instructed to declare war against the Pagan Arabs, i.e., to avenge the wrong inflicted by the latter who had fought the Muslims, driven them out of their homes, and persecuted them for professing Islam.

The final verse, 2:193, prescribes the objective of war as the neutralization of the oppressive forces that prevent people from choosing their belief and religion. It is clear from this verse that war should be carried out against the individuals and institutions that practice oppression and persecute people; not to force and coerce people into Islam. The same verse, therefore, instructs the Muslims to terminate the fighting as soon as this goal has been achieved. In other words, the previous four verses prescribe fighting only against oppressors and tyrants who use force to prevent people from freely professing or practicing their religion.

Let us now examine the verses of *Surat al-Tawbah,* which some Muslim jurists consider to be the final words of the Qur'an concerning the principles governing the initiation of war vis-à-vis non-Muslims. Jurists are divided as to whether these verses abrogate other Qur'anic verses that address the initiation of war. Those who claim that these verses abrogate other verses on the subject base their judgment on the grounds that the verses embody general rules which cancel any other preceding rules. The abrogation, thus, is not predicated on textual evidence (*naṣṣ*), but rather on reasoning and speculation. It follows that the question of abrogation is a matter of opinion and, as such, is subject to discussion and refutation. "If there exists a dispute among the Muslim scholars as to whether a specific rule is subject to abrogation," al-Ṭabarī explains, "we cannot determine that the rule is abrogated unless evidence is presented."[12] Needless to say, al-Ṭabarī means by evidence, a statement provided by the Qur'an or the Sunnah [the tradition of the Prophet] in support of the claim of abrogation. Otherwise the evidence is but another scholar's opinion.

The verses of *Surat al-Tawbah* explicitly declare that the Muslims are to fight the polytheists until they embrace Islam:

> ... slay the *mushrikīn* [polytheists] wherever you find them, and seize them, beleaguer them, and lie in wait for them in every stratagem [of war]; but if they repent, and establish salah and pay zakah, then open the way for them ... (9:5)

The word *mushrikīn* (sing. *mushrik)* in this context indicates specifically the Pagan Arabs[13], as it can be inferred from the first verse, which reads:

> A declaration of disavowal from God and His Messenger to those of the *mushrikīn* with whom you contracted a mutual alliance. (9:1)

The reason for this all-out war against the Pagan Arabs was their continual fight and conspiracy against the Muslims to turn them out of Madinah as they had been turned out of Makkah, and their infidelity to and disregard for the covenant they had made with the Muslims: "Why will you not fight people who violated their oaths, plotted to expel the Messenger, and attacked you first ... " (9:13).

It could be said that what matters here is not the specific circumstances of the revelation, but the general implication of the text, as it is generally accepted in the principles of Islamic jurisprudence (*uṣūl al-fiqh*). The response to this argument is that the particularity (*takhṣīs*) of the previous verse is determined not by the circumstance of its revelation, but by its intent (*ḥikmah al-naṣṣ*), which is also generally acceptable for limiting the application of the text.

ʿAbd al-Wahhāb Khallāf wrote:

> It should be noticed, that the intent of the text is to be distinguished from the circumstance of its revelation, for Muslim jurisprudents are in consensus [*ijmā'*] that the intent of the text may be used for limiting its application, with no dissension by any of them, while the circumstance of its revelation is what they refer to when they say: "What matters is the general implication of the text, not the circumstance of its revelation."[14]

Therefore, the verses 1–14 of *Surat al-Tawbah* can be applied only to Pagan Arabs who lived at the time of the Prophet. The reason they had to be coerced into Islam was that they were hostile to Muslims and had disregarded their oaths and plotted against the Islamic state in Madinah. This understanding is reinforced by the verse 9:4 exempting those who were faithful to their treaties with the Muslims:

> [But the treaties are] not dissolved with those Pagans with whom you have entered into covenant and who have not subsequently failed you in aught; nor aided anyone against you. So fulfill your agreements with them to the end of their term: for God loves the righteous. (9:4)

The previous argument can also be applied to the hadith: "I have been commanded to fight people until they declare that there is no god but God." The word "people" here implies the Pagan Arabs only. For if the word is interpreted to be all-inclusive, the rule embodied in this hadith should also be applied to the Byzantine Christians and the Persian Zoroastrians (*Majūs*). But, since this is not the case, the word "people" has an exclusive meaning and implicates only the Pagan Arabs. This explication is supported by another hadith reported by ʿAbdullah ibn ʿUmar ibn al-Khaṭṭāb, who narrated that the Prophet said:

> I have been commanded to fight people until they declare that there is no deity but God and that Muhammad is the Messenger of God, establish the salah, and pay the zakah. If they do that, their lives and property are inviolable to me, except [in the case when] the [law of] Islam allows me [to take them]. They will be answerable to God.[15]

Clearly the word "People" here implies only the Pagan Arabs who, according to *Surat al-Tawbah*, are to be forced to accept Islam. For obviously the word cannot be considered to include all people, since that contradicts the Qur'anic directions, as well as the practice of the Prophet, which permit the "People of the Book" to maintain their religion. Regarding the word "people" to be all-inclusive will, therefore, violate the provisions that have been given to the "People of the Book" by the Qur'an and the Sunnah.

Abū Ḥanīfa and his pupil Abū Yūsuf contend that only Pagan Arabs are to be coerced into Islam. In his book *Al-Kharāj,* Abū Yūsuf relates that Muḥammad ibn al-Ḥasan said:

> The Prophet, peace be on him, consummated a peace treaty with the Zoroastrians of al-Hajar on the terms that they paid *jizyah,* but did not permit [Muslims] to take their women in marriage or to eat their slaughtered animals.[16]

He also stated that *jizyah* could be collected from all polytheists, such as Zoroastrians, Pagans, Fire and Stone Worshipers, and Sabians, but not from apostates or Pagan Arabs, for the latter groups were to be coerced into Islam.[17] Al-Shāfiʿī and Mālik also contend that *jizyah* can be taken from polytheists.[18]

WAR OF RECONCILIATION

We have seen in the foregoing discussion that the war of domination in which people are to be coerced into Islam involved a particular ruling (*ḥukm khāṣṣ*) limited to the Pagan Arabs, for their hostility and infidelity. Most leading jurists, including Abū Ḥanīfah and his two renowned students Abū Yūsuf and Muḥammad ibn al-Ḥasan, as well as al-Shāfiʿī and Mālik, advocate only the war of reconciliation, in which the "People of the Book" and non-Arab polytheists can enter into peaceful treaties with Muslims, provided that they pay an annual tribute of *jizyah* to the Islamic state. The war of reconciliation is therefore considered by these jurists as a general rule applicable to all non-Muslims. Muslim jurists, thus, divide the world into two territories, *dār al-Islām* and *dār al-Ḥarb,* and declare that a permanent state of war exists between the two until *dār al-Ḥarb* is annexed to *dār al-Islām*. This understanding is founded on verse 29 of *Surat al-Tawbah*.

> Fight those who believe not in God nor the last day, nor forbid what God and His Messenger forbade, nor acknowledge the religion of Truth, [even if they are] of the "People of the Book," until they pay the *jizyah* with willing submission and feel themselves subdued. (9:29)

The first outstanding remark about the verse is that it is not all-inclusive, and thus, does not render a general rule. The verse posits four criteria for those who are to be fought among the "People of the Book:" those who do not believe in God, do not believe in the last day, do not forbid that which is forbidden by God and his Messenger, and do not acknowledge the religion of truth. The verse, obviously, has not been phrased in a way that would implicate the "People of the Book" as a whole,[19] but in a way that sets aside a particular group of the "People of the Book."

The general rule (*ḥukm ʿām*) was derived by the Muslim jurists by *explication de texte* (*ta'wīl al-naṣṣ*). Al-Māwardī, for example, implicates the "People of the Book" by arguing:

> As to the saying of God Almighty "those who believe not in God," [the statement is inclusive of the "People of the Book"] because, although acknowledging the Oneness of God, their belief [in God] could be refuted by one of two explications: First, [by saying that] they do not believe in the Book of God, which is the Qur'an. Second, [by saying that] they do not believe in the prophethood of Muhammad, peace be on him, for acknowledging the prophets is part of the belief in God who commissioned them.[20]

It is clear that al-Māwardī's reasoning stems from neither the letter of the text, nor from its spirit. Rather, the argument presented by al-Māwardī, as well as other classical jurists, has been influenced by the factual circumstances and practical conditions, a question discussed at some length below.

From the foregoing discussion we can conclude that the phraseology of the verse 9:29 provides a particular rule (*ḥukm khāṣṣ*); i.e., war in this verse is prescribed against a particular group of the "People of the Book" because of the four criteria cited above. We can also conclude that the extension of the application of these criteria to the "People of the Book" as a whole is not based on textual evidence (*naṣṣ*) but on reasoning and argumentations; and that the interpretation provided by classical jurists is debatable. Nevertheless, I will not attempt here to reinterpret the verse in consideration, nor will I go into the lengthy discussion as to whether the four criteria may implicate the "People of the Book" in general, because it will be shown later that the Prophet, as well as the first generations of Muslims, did not extend these criteria to the "People of the Book" as a whole. Instead, I will elaborate on the condition, which obligates the Muslims to terminate their offensive against the "People of the Book:" "Until they pay *jizyah* with willing submission and feel themselves subdued."

Jizyah was not levied on the "People of the Book" for the purpose of increasing the income of the Muslim state or promoting the wealth of the Muslim community. Nor was it levied to place a financial burden on non-Muslim individuals and force them to accept Islam; for the amount of *jizyah* was very minimal and levied only on financially solvent males, while exempting women, children, monks, or poor non-Muslims.[21] Rather, *jizyah* attained historically a symbolic meaning as it aimed at subduing hostile states and oppressive regimes so as to assure Muslims that they could promote Islam in that community, and to assure non-Muslims that they could profess Islam without being persecuted or harassed.

Al-Sarakhsī proclaims:

> The purpose of *jizyah*, is not the money, but rather the invitation to Islam in the best manner. Because, by establishing a peace treaty [with non-Muslims], war ceases and security is assured for the peaceful [non-Muslim], who, consequently, has the opportunity to live among the Muslims, experience first-hand the beauty of Islam, or receives admonition, which could lead him to embrace Islam.[22]

In other words, *jizyah* was intended to assure freedom of expression for Muslims to promote Islam in non-Muslim territories, and freedom of belief to those who may choose to embrace Islam. Because *jizyah* was aimed at turning hostile territories into friendly ones, the Muslims did not collect *jizyah* from those who expressed a friendly attitude toward them, or entered a mutual alliance with them, pledging thereby their military support. Al-Ṭabarī, for example, reported in his treatise on history that Suayd ibn Muqrin entered into an agreement with a non-Muslim community, which read in part: "Whoever of you provides services to us will get his reward rather than paying *jizyah*, and you are secure in your lives, property, and religion, and no one can change the provisions of this agreement."[23] Surāqah ibn ʿAmr, likewise, signed a treaty with the Armenians in 22 AH/642 AC, in which the latter were exempted from paying *jizyah* for supporting the Muslims militarily.[24] Ḥabīb ibn Muslimah al-Fahrī, the deputy of Abū ʿUbaydah, also signed a treaty with the Antakians in which the latter were exempted from *jizyah* in return for services and help rendered to the Muslims.[25]

It was also reported in *Futūḥ al-Buldān* that:

> Muʿāwiyah ibn Abī Sufyān signed a treaty with the Armenians in which the institution of religion, the political order, and the judicial system of the latter were left intact, and the Armenians were further released from *jizyah* duties for three years; after that they could either pay an amount of *jizyah* as they chose, or, if they did not wish to pay *jizyah*, prepare fifteen thousand warriors to help the Muslims and to protect the Armenian land. Muʿāwiyah pledged to provide logistical support, should they be attacked by the Byzantines.[26]

It is clear from the foregoing examples that the early Muslims regarded *jizyah* as a measure for neutralizing hostile political communities and opening their territories to Muslims, and not a measure for dominating them or placing financial burdens on them. The previous perception of the real intent of *jizyah* is demonstrable, in a yet clearer fashion, in the friendly relations between the Islamic state and Ethiopia during the early Islamic epochs.

PEACEFUL COEXISTENCE: ABYSSINIA AND ISLAM

The relationship between Abyssinia and the early Islamic state is an excellent case study for rebutting the classical conception of the two territories (*dār al-Islām* and *dār al-Ḥarb*), which calls for a permanent war against non-Muslim political communities until they accept Islam or pay *jizyah*. Mālik ibn Anas, the founder of the Maliki school of law, advised that the Muslims should not conquer Abyssinia, predicating his opinion on the hadith of the Prophet: "Leave the Abyssinians in peace so long as they leave you in peace." He acknowledged that he was not sure of the authenticity of the statement, but said: "People still avoid attacking them."[27] Abyssinia had maintained its Christian identity long after Islam was established in Arabia and North Africa. Few Muslim families could be found in the fourth century AH.[28] From the beginning, Abyssinians showed their goodwill to the early Muslims who, escaping the persecution of Quraysh, had sought refuge in

Abyssinia. The Muslim émigrés were welcomed by the Abyssinians and were further protected from their persecutors who sent a delegation to bring the Muslim escapees back home. Good relations between Abyssinia and the Islamic state continued, the former being the only nation to acknowledge Islam at that time.[29]

The peaceful relationship between Abyssinia and the Islamic state is very significant for rebutting the concept of the two territorial divisions of the world, and its corollary conception of a permanent state of war which does not permit the recognition of any non-Muslim state as a sovereign entity and insists that the latter should always pay a tribute to the Islamic state. For although Abyssinia had never been a Muslim nation, it was recognized by the early Islamic state as an independent state that could be let alone without imposing any kind of tax on it or forcing it into the orbit of the Islamic state. Obviously, Abyssinia could not be considered a part of the territory of Islam (*dār al-Islam*), for Islamic rule had never been exacted therein;[30] nor would it be considered a part of the territory of war (*dār al-Ḥarb*), since there had been no attempt to force it into the pale of Islam or to declare a permanent war against it. The only satisfactory explanation of the peculiar position of Abyssinia is that the doctrine of the two territories was founded on a fragile basis. Some Muslim sources claim that al-Najāshī, the king of Abyssinia during the time of the Prophet, had embraced Islam after receiving the invitation of the Prophet.[31] Ibn al-Athīr, for instance, wrote in this regard:

> When al-Najāshī received the letter of the Prophet, he believed in him, following his [instructions], and embraced Islam in the presence of Ja'far ibn Abū Ṭālib, then sent sixty Abyssinians to the Prophet headed by his son; the group had drowned however while sailing [to Madinah].[32]

The story about al-Najāshī's accepting Islam did not affect the status of Abyssinia as a territory in which Islam did not rule, and, consequently, should be considered, according to the definition of classical writers, a territory of war.[33]

CHAPTER TWO

ISLAM AND PEACE

A SYSTEMATIC examination of Islamic texts and Muslim history show that peace is and has always been the original position and final aim of Islam. War can and must be fought, however, to repel aggression and lift oppression, but only as the last resort. War should not be seen as an instrument of the state to advance ideological commitments of the bearers of political power.

We argue in this chapter that peace must be the governing principle of political action, both locally and globally. War is not, and should never be, a political choice. War in Islam has specific objectives, and these objectives revolve around defending human rights against brutal force. Advancing narrow interests and imposing religious beliefs are not legitimate objectives of war in Islam.

PEACE IS THE ESSENCE

From its inception, the Qur'an emphasized peace as an intrinsic Islamic value. In fact, the terms "Islam" and "peace" have the same root, *salām*. Furthermore, God has chosen the word peace (*salām*) as the Muslim's greeting. Reviewing the early Muslim era and reflecting on the experience of the early Muslim generations, one can clearly see that peace was always the original position of Muslims, and that war was either a punitive measure to repel tyranny and oppression, or a defensive measure to stop aggression.

From the very beginning, Prophet Muhammad was instructed to use a friendly and polite approach to call people to Islam.

> Invite to the way of your Lord with wisdom and beautiful preaching; and argue with them in ways that are best and most gracious. (16:125)

Despite the violent opposition of the Quraysh, the Prophet proceeded to summon people peacefully to Islam, and the Muslims were further commanded, for prudential reasons, not to respond to the violence of the Quraysh. As it will be discussed in more detail below, Muslim pacifism during the Makkan period was a political choice to effect peaceful change and to protect the community from self-destruction.

After the emigration to Madinah, the Muslims were permitted to fight against those who declared war against them.

> To those against whom war is made, permission is given [to fight], because they are wronged; and verily, God is most Powerful for their aid; [they are] those who have been expelled from their homes in defiance of right, for no cause except that they say, "our Lord is God." (22:39–40)

As a result, the Muslims fought a series of battles against the Quraysh, including the Battles of Badr and Uḥud. The situation was further escalated when other Arab tribes joined with the Quraysh in the war against the infant Islamic state of Madinah in an attempt to destroy it. The campaign to eliminate the Muslims reached its climax in the Battle of al-Khandaq (The Trench) when ten thousand fighters of the Quraysh and their allies surrounded Madinah.[34] The Muslims, none the less, made several attempts to neutralize their foes by signing a peace treaty with the Quraysh and their allies at al-Ḥudaybiyyah.[35] Unfortunately, the Arab tribesman of the Quraysh and their allies, who had thrived historically on war and developed, consequently, a warlike culture, did not respect the treaty and violated its provisions. It became, thus, quite clear that the only way to neutralize these people was by annulling the cultural basis of their hostility and infidelity, which could be done only by coercing them into Islam.

The original position of the Muslims concerning the Jews of Madinah was also based on the principle of peaceful coexistence. A few months after the Prophet arrived in Madinah, he concluded a covenant of friendship, alliance, and cooperation between the Muhājirūn and the Anṣār on one side and the Jews on the other.[36]

The covenant not only recognized the freedom of religion of the Jews and assured their security, but also provided them with complete autonomy, bound with certain duties and obligations, mutually applicable on both Jews and Muslims, as the following excerpt of the document reads:

> ... As the Jews fight on the side of the Muslims, they shall spend of their wealth on equal par with the Muslims. The Jews have their religion and the Muslims theirs. Both enjoy the security of their own populace and clients except the unjust and the criminal among them. The unjust or the criminal destroys only himself and his family.[37]

The friendly relationship between the Jews of Madinah and the Muslims continued until ʿAbdullāh ibn Salām, a rabbi and a prominent Jewish leader, embraced Islam. This incident, evidently, sparked grave panic among Jewish leaders, who became apprehensive about the Muslim presence in Madinah and feared that Islam would penetrate their ranks. It was at this stage that Jews began their campaign against Muslims; first through a war of words, aimed at refuting the Qur'anic teaching and inducing a state of suspicion about the Prophet and his message, and later through conspiring with the enemies of Islam.[38]

The first confrontation between Jews and Muslims took place after the Battle of Badr when some Jews of Banū Qaynuqāʿ violated the right of a Muslim women by forcefully exposing her nakedness. This incident developed into fighting between a Muslim passerby and the Jewish assailants in which a Jew and the passerby were killed. Consequently, general fighting between the clan of the murdered Muslim and Banū Qaynuqāʿ erupted. When the Prophet was informed of the confrontation, he sent word to Banū Qaynuqāʿ, asking them to stop the attacks and keep the covenant of mutual peace and security. Banū Qaynuqāʿ responded by ridiculing the Prophet's request, leaving the Muslims no option but to fight.[39]

Likewise, the campaign against Banū al-Naḍīr was triggered by their infidelity and misconduct, when they openly violated the provisions of their covenant with the Muslims by sending three of their leaders, Ḥuyayy ibn Akhṭab, Salām ibn Abū al-Ḥuqayq, and Kinānah ibn al-Ḥuqyaq, together with two leaders of the tribe of Banū Wā'il, to Makkah in order to instigate the Quraysh and their allies to attack the Muslims in Madinah, and to pledge their support. Indeed, the Jewish delegation was able to mobilize the Pagan Arabs against the Muslims, and their counsel led to the campaign of al-Khandaq, invoking the most horrible experience that the Muslims had ever had in their struggle against the Quraysh and their allies.[40]

In like manner, the fighting between the Islamic state and both Byzantium and Persia was commenced not because the Muslims wanted to extend the dominion of the Islamic state, or *dār al-Islām,* using the classical terminology, but rather because both the Byzantines and the Persians either assailed Muslim individuals and caravans or prevented the communication of the Islamic message.

The campaign of Dawmah al-Jandal, the first campaign against the northern Christian tribes which were Byzantine protectorates, was a punitive expedition to avenge the attacks on the Muslim caravans to al-Shām (Syria) by some of these tribes, such as Qaḍā'ah and Banū Kalb.[41]

Likewise, the campaign of Mu'tah was also a punitive expedition to avenge several grave violations against the Muslim messengers and missionaries whom Muhammad had sent north to call people to Islam and introduce the new faith to the northern regions. For example, the Prophet sent al-Ḥārith ibn ʿUmayr to the governor of Busrah. Upon reaching Mu'tah, al-Ḥārith met with Sharhabīl Amir ibn al-Ghassanī, who asked him, "are you a messenger of Muhammad?" Al-Ḥārith answered: "Yes." Then Sharhabīl ordered his men to kill him, and he was executed.[42]

> [The Prophet also sent] five men to Banū Sulaymān for the sole purpose of teaching them Islam, and he endured their cold blooded murder by their hosts. Only their leader managed to escape, and he did so purely accidentally. The Prophet also sent fifteen men to Dhāt al-Ṭalḥ on the outskirts of al-Shām in order to call its people

> to Islam. There, too, the messengers of Muhammad and the missionaries of faith were put to death in cold blood.[43]

It was also reported that the northern Christian tribes killed those among them who had professed Islam,[44] leaving the Muslims, therefore, no choice but to fight them for their aggression and tyranny. These incidents, and others, triggered the campaigns of Mu'tah and al-Ḥudaybiyyah, and led eventually to the conquest of al-Shām and Iraq.

Evidently, the doctrine of the two territorial division of the world, and its corollary concept of the permanent state of war, was influenced by the factual conditions that existed during the period when this conception was conceived, namely the hostile relations between the Abbasid Caliphate and Byzantine Empire. The jurists who devised the classical doctrine had, obviously, overlooked not only the peaceful coexistence between the early Islamic state and Abyssinia, but also the earlier hostility of Byzantium and its allies against the emerging Islamic state.[45] Muhammad Abu Zahrah wrote protesting the classical doctrine:

> We object to including this division (i.e., *dār al-Islām* and *dār al-Ḥarb*) in the Muslim legal theory as one of its principles. As a matter of fact, this division under the Abbasids corresponded to the factual relations between the Islamic state and non-Islamic state. Classical writers only intended to give a legal justification to that situation.[46]

RESPECTING INDIVIDUAL FREEDOM OF BELIEF

We concluded in the foregoing discussion that, contrary to the claims of the classical doctrine of the territorial division of the world, war is not the instrument of the Islamic state to propagate Islam and extend its territory. We turn now to examine a question that closely relates to the previous argumentation: Does Islam recognize individual freedom of conscience, i.e., are people free to accept or reject Islam? And if the answer is yes, how can we explain the fact that the Muslims fought the apostates (*murtaddūn*) during the administration of Abū Bakr?

The answer to the first question is an emphatic yes. The principle of the freedom of belief has been unequivocally established in two Qur'anic verses:

> If it had been the Lord's will, all those who are on earth would have believed; will you then compel mankind, against their will, to believe? (10:99)

> Let there be no compulsion in religion: Truth stands out clear from error. (2:256)

The first verse was revealed in Makkah before Hijrah, while the second was revealed in Madinah after Hijrah. As al-Qurṭubī mentioned in his Qur'anic commentary, *Al-Jāmiᶜ Li Aḥkām al-Qur'ān,* some commentators claim that the second verse has been abrogated by the verses of *Surat al-Tawbah,* which permitted the Muslims to fight the "People of the Book," while others ascertain that it has not been abrogated. Al-Qurṭubī quotes Abū Jaᶜfar's interpretation of this verse: "The meaning of 'let there be no compulsion in religion' is that no one is to be forced to accept Islam. The *al* has been added to the world *dīn* so that their combination, *al-dīn,* would indicate Islam."[47]

Nor can this principle be abrogated by the hadith: "I have been commanded to fight people until they say: 'There is no god but God.'" For as it was indicated above, the hadith embodies a particular rule (*ḥukm khāṣṣ*) which is applicable only to the Pagan Arabs. Even if we were to hypothetically treat the hadith as a general rule, it could not be used to abrogate a Qur'anic verse. For while the previous hadith is an exclusively narrated hadith (*ḥadīth āḥād*) and therefore uncertain *(ẓannī al-dalālah),* the verse, like all other Qur'anic verses, is extensively narrated (*mutawātir*) and, therefore, certain (*qaṭᶜī al-dalālah*).[48]

The claim of abrogation is clearly flawed, for both verses embody a firm rule (*muḥkam*).[49] The first verse points out in unequivocal fashion that it had not been God's will that mankind should be forced to believe; and the second verse provides more explanation as to why people should not be compelled to accept Islam by indicating that "Truth stands out clear from error." Because God's will is not subject to change, and because truth stands always clear from error, the two verses are not, therefore, subject to abrogation.[50]

But if the general rule is that no one is to be forced to accept Islam, how should Muslims deal with the question of apostasy (*riddah*)? The classical position concerning the apostates is that they should be killed. This position is predicated primarily on two pieces of evidence: the jihad of Muslims, under the leadership of Abū Bakr, against the Arab apostates, and the hadith: "The blood of a Muslim may not be legally spilt other than in three instances: the married person who commits adultery; a life for a life; and one who forsakes his religion and abandons the community (*jamāʿah*)."[51]

We should distinguish, when dealing with the question of apostasy, between two different cases. First, when a collectivity of people revolt against the Muslim authorities and refuse to obey the law of Islam, as was the case of the apostates (*murtaddūn*) who refused to pay zakah to Abū Bakr and mobilized their forces to prevent him from collecting it. These apostates are to be fought, not because of their rejection of Islam, but because of their rebellion against and disobedience to the law. The war against them can, thus, be considered a law-enforcement war. Second, when an individual refuses to fulfill one of his public obligations, such as a person who refuses to pay zakah to the Muslim authorities, he is to be compelled to pay it, according to the opinion of the majority of the Muslim jurists – not to be fought or killed. Only when he violently resists the Muslim authorities, and uses force of arms to prevent them from discharging their duties and imposing the law, can he be fought against.[52]

The above-cited hadith vividly states that the individual apostate could be killed not merely because of his rejection of Islam, but because of his rebellion and revolt against the Muslim community. In other words, a quiet desertion of personal Islamic duties is not a sufficient reason for inflicting death on a person. Only when the individual's desertion of Islam is used as a political tool for instigating a state of disorder, or revolting against the law of Islam, can the individual apostate then be put to death as a just punishment for his act of treason and betrayal of the Muslim community.

The war against the apostates is carried out not to force them to accept Islam, but to enforce the Islamic law and maintain order. Therefore, the individual apostasy, which takes place quietly and without causing any public disorder, should not be of concern to the Islamic authority. Only when the individual openly renounces Islam and violates Islamic law, should he be punished for breaking the law and challenging the norms and beliefs of the Muslim community; and only when a group of people revolt against the Muslim authority, and refuse to implement the Islamic law in the area it controls – by failing, for instance, to establish public prayers, or by abolishing the institution of zakah – can the Islamic authority declare war against them. It follows that if a group of Muslims oppose certain views widely accepted by the general public or protest certain decisions made by the public authority, they are not to be fought as long as they do not violate the Islamic law or pose a threat to the Islamic state – i.e., by initiating war against Muslims or allying themselves with their enemies. When the Kharijites (Khawārij) opposed ʿAlī ibn Abū Ṭālib and refused to recognize his authority, confronting him with the slogan: "authority is only from God," he did not declare war against them and stated that they could claim three rights: "Not to be prevented from attending mosques, not to be preemptively attacked, and not to be denied their share of booty so long as they fight with us."[53] "If an opposing group revolted against a just community," al-Māwardī wrote, "and controlled a region, making it their exclusive territory, the group cannot be fought so long as they do not violate any rights or disobey the general law."[54]

CHAPTER THREE

THE LIMITS OF WAR

WE CONCLUDED, in the foregoing discussion, that the aim of war is not to propagate or spread Islam, nor is it to expand the territory of the Islamic state or dominate, politically or militarily, non-Muslim regions. Rather, the aim of war is to establish and assure justice, and to annihilate oppression and abolish tyranny. It is true that the right to communicate the message of Islam is protected under Islamic law, and the Islamic state must, therefore, respect and defend this right. But the obligation to protect the right of Muslims, and for this matter all religious communities, to promote their belief and values should be carried out through peaceful means and in a friendly manner. The assurance of justice and destruction of tyranny are therefore the underlying objectives of war. However, since the terms "justice" and "tyranny" cover wide ground and permit broad interpretation, they need to be translated into more concrete forms. We can distinguish four situations where the violation of the principle of justice and the excessive misconduct of tyranny call the Islamic state to war and justify its use of violence against the political entity that is implicated in such practices.

1. WAR AGAINST OPPRESSION

It is incumbent upon Muslims to challenge any political authority that either prohibits the free exchange of ideas, or prevents people from freely professing or practicing the religion that they chose to embrace.

> And fight them until there is no more persecution and religion is only for God ... (2:193)

> And why should ye not fight in the cause of God and of those who, being weak, are oppressed – men, women, and children, whose cry is: "Our Lord, rescue us from this town, whose people are oppressors; and raise for us from Thee one who will protect; and raise for us from Thee one who will help." (4:75)

It should be made clear here that the oppression by a particular regime is not to be determined by comparing the values and conduct of that regime with Islamic norms and standard, but rather by its respect for basic human dignity and freedom: freedom to choose one's religion, freedom to communicate one's values and beliefs, and freedom to associate with a community of one's choosing. Corruption and mismanagement should not be considered, therefore, the criteria that classify a particular regime as oppressive, deserving, thus, to be fought, because, it may be recalled, Muslims are commanded to invite mankind to Islam through friendly means and effect social and political change using the peaceful methods of education and moral reformation. Only when their peaceful efforts are frustrated and met with violence, are they justified in using violence to subdue the aggressive party. As it was shown above, the Prophet did not resort to war against the Pagan Arabs until they persecuted the Muslims and violated their lives and properties; nor did he fight the Jews of Madinah until they betrayed the Muslims and conspired with their enemies. Similarly, the Prophet declared war against Byzantium and its Arab allies only when they killed the messengers and missionaries who were sent to peacefully summon people to Islam and introduce to them the new revelation of God.

2. WAR IN DEFENSE OF MUSLIM INDIVIDUALS AND PROPERTY

When wrong is inflicted on a Muslim individual by a member, or members, of another political community, whether this wrong is done to his person, by assaulting or murdering him, or to his property by robbing or unjustly confiscating it, the Islamic state is obligated to make sure the individual, or his family, is compensated for his suffering, and that his rights are upheld. Because it is beyond the scope of this paper to discuss the legal procedure of this matter, it suffices to say that the Islamic state should ensure that justice has been done to the wronged Muslim, even if it means a declaration of war against the political community that tolerates such an aggression, provided that the authority of the political community has refused to amend the wrong inflicted on the Muslim individual after it has been formally notified and given a reasonable time in which to respond.

> ... Whoever then acts aggressively against you, inflict injury on him according to the injury he has inflicted on you and be careful [of your duty] to God and know that God is with those who guard [against evil]. (2:194)

3. WAR AGAINST FOREIGN AGGRESSION

The clear-cut case of foreign aggression is a military attack on the Islamic state or its allies. The Muslims, however, are not obliged to wait until the enemies launch their attack, before responding. Rather, the Islamic state can initiate war and carry out a preemptive strike if the Muslim authorities become convinced beyond a shadow of a doubt that the enemy is mobilizing its forces and is about to carry out an offensive, or if a state of war already exists between the Islamic state and its adversaries.

If aggression is committed against another political entity with which the Islamic state has entered into mutual alliance, or has signed a treaty that stipulates military protection, the Islamic state is also obliged to fulfill its commitment to its ally and provide the military support needed. The conquest of Makkah was precipitated by the Quraysh's attack on Khuzāʿah, which was an ally of the Islamic city-state of Madinah, violating thereby a provision of the Treaty of al-Ḥudaybiyyah that prohibited such an act.[55]

4. WAR OF LAW ENFORCEMENT

When a proportion of the population residing within the boundaries of the Islamic state violently oppose the application of the

Islamic law, or threaten the territorial integrity of the Islamic state, the Muslim authorities are justified in using armed force to subdue the rebellion. It should be emphasized, however, that what is at issue here is not just opposition to a particular public policy, but an insurrection that attempts to achieve its goals through military tactics, threatening thereby the lives and property of other members of the society. Three types of dissension, however, should be differentiated, two of which are merely causes of rebellion, which can be forcefully subdued, while the third is a case of legitimate political opposition that should be dealt with in a peaceful manner.

a) *Apostasy*

When a group of Muslim individuals fortify themselves in an area of the Muslim territory and refuse to permit the application in the territory they control of certain fundamental Islamic practices or laws, such as the establishment of public prayer (*salah al-jamā*ᶜ*ah*), the payment of zakah, and the like, it is a case of apostasy, for which the group is to be fought until its members cease their rebellion and allow other Muslims to practice Islamic law. It should be clear that apostates are to be fought not because they refuse to profess or practice Islam, but because they disobey the law and subvert public order. Therefore, nobody should be questioned or prosecuted for not fulfilling his personal duties toward God – for he is answerable to God, not the Muslim community in so far as his personal duties are concerned – as long as he fulfills his public duty. For example, the individual who privately neglects prayer is not subject to any punitive measures, so long as he does not publicly denounce prayer. Nor can he be forced to attend public prayers because attending congregations is a voluntary duty and matter of personal choice. He can, however, be forced to pay zakah, and can be punished for refusing to render his share to the Muslim authority because zakah is not only a personal duty, but a public obligation as well.

b) *Insurrection*

When a group of Muslim individuals fortify themselves in an area of the Muslim territory, then refuse to implement a public policy formulated by just authority and through due procedure, and use the force of arms to prevent the authorities from taking into custody and prosecuting those who do not comply with public policy, it is a case of insurrection which justifies the use of armed force by the Muslim authority to subdue the rebellion.

c) *Political Opposition*
When a group of Muslim individuals peacefully oppose a public policy, use a public forum to object to its application, and attempt to persuade the rest of the population to adopt their view regarding this policy, it is a case of political opposition which does not justify the use of force by the authority to circumscribe the influence of the opposition or to destroy it. The authority can, if it perceives that the opposition constitutes a threat to the general welfare, respond by initiating legal proceedings through the courts or by inducing sanctions through the institution of *al-shūrā* (consultation), or by using any other peaceful measures that the general law of the Islamic state permits.

PEACE AND THE STATE OF WAR

Peace in Islam does not mean the absence of war, but the absence of oppression and tyranny. Islam considers that real peace can be attained only when justice prevails. Islam, therefore, justifies war against regimes that prevent people from choosing their ideals and practicing their beliefs. It does not, however, justify war against non-Muslim entities that neither prevent the preaching of Islam nor inflict wrong upon Muslims. The Islamic state should thus maintain peace with those who show goodwill to Muslims. The Islamic state is justified, on the other hand, in declaring war against those who commit aggression against it or its mission. "This movement," Sayyid Qutb wrote, "uses the methods of preaching and persuasion for reforming ideas and belief, and uses physical power and jihad for abolishing the organizations and authorities of the *jāhilī* system which prevents people from reforming their ideas and beliefs ...."[56]

The classical jurists, who devised the doctrine of two division, *dār al-Islām* and *dār al-Ḥarb,* indiscriminately classify all non-Muslim communities in one category and advocate a permanent state of war against them, insisting that Muslims should not establish peaceful relations unless they are forced to.[57] Clearly, this doctrine, which reflects the factual relationship between the Islamic and non-Islamic states during the Abbasid era, fails to take into account the total principles as well as the real objectives of the Ummah. As Ibn Taymiyyah points out in his book *Al-Siyāsah al-Sharʿīyyah,* fighting against non-Muslims is not the aim of the Islamic state, but fighting can be employed against those who deny Muslims the right to carry out their mission – the propagation of Islam.

> Fighting has been permitted so that the object of making the religion only for God and making the Word of God supreme can be advanced. It has been agreed that whoever prevents [the Muslims from carrying out] this [mission] is to be fought. But those who do not fight [against the Muslims] such as women, children, monks, elderly, the blind and the crippled, and the like, except when they fight by words and actions, should not be killed, according to the majority of scholars. Some [scholars] however, argue that all [unbelievers] should be killed because of their blasphemy – except women and children, because they are Muslim property.[58] Only the first argument, however, is correct, because fighting is [permitted] against those who fight us to prevent us from calling [people] to the religion of God. As the Almighty said: "Fight in the cause of God those who fight you, but do not commit aggression, for God loves not aggressors" (2:190).

As Ibn Taymiyyah states:

> God has permitted taking life only in so far as it is necessary to promote righteousness and good behavior. ...Therefore, any [unbeliever] who does not prevent Muslims from practicing the religion of God, he hurts by his disbelief no one but his own soul.[59]

Subsuming of all non-Muslims under one label and declaring

a permanent state of war against them all is unjustified and completely wrong. It is true that a state of war may exist between the Islamic state and a hostile power, but hostility should be evident before the state of war is declared. The Muslims, therefore, should distinguish between the peaceful and the hostile and treat each accordingly. This distinction has been made by the Qur'an; and subsequently by Prophet Muhammad and his Companions, long before the doctrine of the two territorial divisions was articulated. *Surat al-Mumtaḥinah* (verses 8–9) makes it quite clear that non-Muslims are not one category but two, and state that they should be dealt with differently.

> God forbids you not, with regard to those who fight you not for [your] faith, nor drive you out of your homes, from dealing kindly and justly with them. For God loves those who are just. (60:8)

> God only forbids you, with regard to those who fight you for [your] faith, and drive you out of your homes, and support [others] in driving you out, from turning to them [for friendship and protection]. It is such as turn to them [in these circumstances] that do wrong. (60:9)

CHAPTER FOUR

PRINCIPLES AND REALITIES

JIHAD we argued earlier, refers to the efforts one exerts to uphold the principles of right and justice. Jihad may be pursued by words, peaceful action, or war. The question then is when, and according to what method, should jihad be practiced? This chapter aims at addressing this question.

THE PRINCIPLES OF PEACE AND ITS STRATEGY

If war is justified in the situations described in the previous chapter, a question arises as to whether Muslims are obligated to fight in these situation, no matter what the circumstances are, or whether it is simply a matter of permissibility or choice, and hence up to the Muslim community to exercise its right to declare war in such situations. To answer this question we need to differentiate between the principle of jihad as a permanent obligation incumbent upon Muslims, and the method of jihad which is to be determined after assessing prevailing conditions of the moment, and selecting the most appropriate method of jihad to effectively deal with these conditions. In other words, while the Ummah is obliged to uphold the principle of jihad and satisfy its requirements, the method of honoring this principle is a question of strategy. Eliminating oppression and protecting human life, defending Muslim sovereignty and upholding the Islamic law, are objectives of the Ummah. The principle of jihad obligates the Muslims to maintain and achieve these objectives. The best way to achieve these objectives, and the most appropriate method of upholding the principle of jihad are, however, a question of leadership and strategy.

Throughout the Makkan period, the Muslims maintained a

pacifist approach in dealing with their adversaries, despite the physical abuse and mental anguish inflicted upon them by the Quraysh. For pacifism was then the best method to effectively achieve Muslim objectives.[60] Some might argue that the Muslims did not resort to violence during the Makkan period because they were not permitted to fight at that time – an argument easily overturned when we realize that the absence of the principle of self-defense during the Makkan period was a temporary suspension of the principle's application, rather than its nullification or rejection. Certainly, the Qur'an unequivocally states that the principle of self-defense and military deference is an essential element of social life and a fundamental principle on which human civilization has evolved

> ... and had it not been [the Will of God] that one set of people is repelled by another, certainly the earth would have been in a state of disorder. (2:251)

> ... and had it not been [the Will of God] that one set of people is repelled by another, certainly there would have been pulled down monasteries, churches, synagogues, and mosques, in which the name of God is commemorated in abundant measure. (22:40)

Thus, it is up to the Muslim leadership to assess the situation and weigh the circumstances as well as the capacity of the Muslim community before deciding the appropriate type of jihad. At one stage, Muslims may find that jihad through persuasion or peaceful resistance is the best and most effective method to achieve a just peace, as was the case during the Makkan period. At another stage, fortification and defensive tactics may be the best way to achieve these objectives, as was the case of the Battle of al-Khandaq. At yet a third stage, the Muslim leadership may decide that all-out war is the most appropriate measure to bring about just peace, as was the case during the war against the Arab apostates.

The selection of the method of jihad, however, is not an arbitrary decision, but one that takes into account the general conditions of both the Muslim community and its adversaries, including the military balance between the Muslims and their enemies and the morale of the Muslim army. The Qur'an circumscribed the Muslim ability to militarily confront its adversaries by two ratios (ten-to-one and two-to-one) that set the upper and lower limits of the Muslim forces in terms of their manpower.

> O Prophet, rouse the believers to the fight. If there are twenty amongst you, patient and persevering, they will vanquish two hundred: if a hundred, they will vanquish a thousand of the unbelievers: for these are people without understanding. (8:65)

> For the present, God hath lightened your [task], for He knows that there is a weak spot in you: but [even though], if there are a hundred of you, patient and persevering, they will vanquish two hundred, and if a thousand, they will vanquish two thousand, with the leave of God: for God is with those who patiently persevere. (8:66)

These verses vividly state that given favorable conditions and high morale, Muslims could, by virtue of their faith, win against odds of ten to one. But when their organization and equipment are weak, and their morale falls short of the optimal situation, they are obligated to tackle no more than odds of two to one. The first situation was illustrated at the Battle of Badr, where the Muslim army crushed a force threefold bigger, while the second situation is demonstrable in the Battle of al-Khandaq, when Muslims, confronted with a force many times stronger than their own, elected to fortify their city by digging a ditch around Madinah, and thus avoided military confrontation with their enemies.[61]

CONCLUSION

Evidently, the classical doctrine of war and peace has not been predicated on a comprehensive theory. The doctrine describes the factual conditions that historically prevailed between the Islamic state during the Abbasid and Byzantium eras, and thus renders rules which respond to specific historical needs. The lack of a comprehensive theory of war and peace has led further to major errors in perceiving the role of war and the real objectives of the Islamic state vis-à-vis non-Muslim communities.

The classical doctrine mistakenly perceives war as the instrument of the Islamic state to expand the Muslim territories and dominate non-Muslim states. As has been shown in this paper, the aim of war is to assure justice and abolish oppression and tyranny. The promotion of Islam is to be achieved through persuasion and the use of peaceful means, not by force and compulsion. Only when the peaceful effort is frustrated, is the Islamic state justified in resorting to war. Yet a true peace in Islam does not mean the absence of war, because Islam considers that real peace can only be attained when justice prevails. Islam, therefore, justifies war against regimes that prevent people from choosing their ideas or practicing their beliefs.

Finally, although this discussion has been confined to the conception of war and peace and issues concerning the initiation of war, it can also be extended to questions concerning the prosecution of war and the conduct of peace – e.g., treaties, prisoners of war, and so forth. Many of the rules pertaining to these issues are predicated on customs, traditions, or conceptions peculiar to the historical period in which these rules were first articulated, and have thus a historically limited application.

APPENDIX

THE COVENANT OF MADINAH

The Covenant of Madinah (*Ṣaḥīfat al-Madinah*) was written under the direction of the Prophet of Islam, and served as the charter for the first Muslim polity, upon the immigration of the Prophet and his assumption of the highest political authority in the newly founded city-state of Madinah.

The Covenant established the first pluralist political order in which the equal autonomy of multi-religious society were recognized, including the freedom of religion, movement, association, etc.

The Covenant makes it abundantly clear that Islamic morality and code of law are not to be imposed on non-Muslim communities, and that the binding principles for a multi-religious society must recognize the common interests of all.

The text of the Covenant is reproduced in the following pages.

IN THE NAME OF GOD, THE COMPASSIONATE, THE MERCIFUL.

This is a Covenant given by Muhammad to the believers and the Muslims of Quraysh, Yathrib, and those who followed them, joined them, and fought with them. They constitute one Ummah to the exclusion of all others. As was their custom, the Muhajirūn from Quraysh are bound together and shall ransom their prisoners in kindness and justice as believers do. Following their own custom, Banu ʿAwf are bound together as they have been before. Every clan of them shall ransom its prisoners with the kindness and justice common among believers. [The text here repeats the same prescription concerning every clan including Banu al-Ḥārith, Banu Sāʿidah, Banu Jushām, Banu-al Najjār, Banu ʿAmr ibn ʿAwf, and Banu al-Nābit].

The believers shall leave none of their members in destitution without giving him in kindness what he needs by way of ransom or blood wit. No believer shall take as an ally a freedman of another Muslim without the permission of his previous master. All pious believers shall rise as one man against whosoever rebels or seeks to commit injustice, aggression, sin, or spread mutual enmity between the believers, even though he may be one of their sons. No believer shall slay a believer; neither shall he assist an unbeliever against a believer. Just as God's bond is one and indivisible, all believers shall stand behind the commitment of the least of them. All believers are bonded one to another to the exclusion of other men. Any Jew who follows us is entitled to our assistance and the same rights as any one of us, without injustice or partisanship.

This Covenant is one and indivisible. No believer shall enter into a separate peace without all the believers whenever there is fighting in the cause of God, but will do so only on the basis of equality and justice to all others. In every military expedition we undertake our members shall be accompanied by others committed to the same objective. All believers shall avenge the blood of one another whenever any one of them falls fighting in the cause of God. The pious believers follow the best and most upright guidance. No unbeliever shall be allowed to place under his protection against the interest of a believer, any wealth or person belonging to Quryash. Whoever is convicted of killing a believer deliberately but without righteous cause, shall be liable to the relatives of the killed. Until the latter are satisfied, the killer shall be subject to retaliation by each and every believer. The killer shall have no rights whatever until this right of the believers is satisfied.

Whoever has entered into this Covenant and believed in God and in the last day shall never protect or give shelter to a convict or criminal; whoever does so shall be cursed by God and upon him shall the divine wrath fall on the Day of Judgment. Neither repentance nor ransom shall be acceptable from him. No object of contention among you may not be referred to God and to Muhammad – may God's peace and blessing be upon him – for judgment. As the Jews fight on the side of the believers, they shall spend of their wealth on equal par with the believers.

The Jews have their religion and the Muslims theirs. Both enjoy the security of their own populace and clients except the unjust and the criminal among them. The unjust or the criminal destroys only himself and his family. The Jews of Banu al-Najjār, Banu al-Ḥārith, Banu Sāʿidah, Banu Jushām, Banu al-Aws, Banu Thaʿlabah, Jafnah, and Banu al-Shutaybah – to all the same rights and privileges apply as to the Jews of Banu al-Aws. The clients of the tribe of Thaʿlabah enjoy the same rights and duties as the members of the tribe themselves. Likewise, the clients of the Jews as the Jews themselves. None of the foregoing shall go out to war except with the permission of Muhammad – may God's peace and blessing be upon him – though none may be prevented from taking revenge for a wound inflicted upon him. Whoever murders anyone will have murdered himself and the members of his family, unless it be the case of a man suffering a wrong, for God will accept his action.

The Jews shall bear their public expenses and so will the Muslims. Each shall assist the other against any violater of this Covenant. Their relationship shall be one of mutual advice and consultation, and mutual assistance and charity rather than harm and aggression. However, no man is liable to a crime committed by his ally. Assistance is due to the party suffering an injustice, not to the one perpetrating it. Since the Jews fight on the side of the believers they shall spend their wealth on a par with them.

The town of Yathrib shall constitute a sanctuary for the parties of this Covenant. Their neighbors shall be treated as themselves as long as they perpetrate no crime and commit no harm. No woman may be taken under protection without the consent of her family. Whatever difference or dispute between the parties to this Covenant remains unsolved shall be referred to God and to Muhammad, the Prophet of God – may God's peace and blessing be upon him. God is the guarantor of the piety and goodness that is embodied in this Covenant. Neither the Quraysh nor their allies shall be given any protection.

The people of this Covenant shall come to the assistance of one another against whoever attacks Yathrib. If they are called to cease hostilities and to enter into a peace, they shall be bound to do so in the interest of peace. If, on the other hand, they call upon the Muslims to cease hostilities and to enter into a peace, they shall be bound to do so in the interest of peace. If, on the other hand, they call upon the Muslims to cease hostilities and to enter into a peace, the Muslims shall be bound to do so and maintain the peace except when the war is against their religion. To every smaller group belongs the share which is their due as members of the larger group which is party to this Covenant. The Jews of al-Aws, as well as their clients, are entitled to the same rights as this Covenant has granted to its parties together with the goodness and charity of the latter. Charity and goodness are clearly distinguishable from crime and injury, and there is no responsibility except for one's own deeds.

God is the guarantor of the truth and good will of this Covenant. This Covenant shall constitute no protection for the unjust or criminal. Whoever goes out to fight as well as whoever stays at home shall be safe and secure in this city unless he has perpetrated an injustice or committed a crime. God grants His protection to whoever acts in piety, charity, and goodness.

NOTES

[1] Muhammad Talaat al-Ghunaimi, *The Muslim Conception of International Law and the Western Approach* (Netherlands: Martinus Nijhoff/The Hague, 1399/1978). p.156: and Ibn Rushd, Chapter on *Jihad,* in *Bidāyah al-Mujtahid wa Nihayah al-Muqtaṣid,* trans. Rudolph Peters in *Jihad in Mediaeval and Modern Islam* (Belgium: E.J. Brill, 1398/1977), p. 24.

[2] The doctrine has been criticized by some contemporary Muslim scholars, such as Muhammad Abū Zahrah, Maḥmūd Shaltūt, and Muhammad al-Ghunaimi.

[3] Al-Ghunaimi, pp.138–39; and Ibn Rushd, pp.24–25, and 61.

[4] Religion is the translation of the Arabic term *al-dīn*, which also connotes judgment, liability, compliance, and indebtedness.

[5] Zakiyy al-Dīn al-Mundhirī, ed., *Mukhtaṣar Ṣaḥīḥ Muslim,* ed. Nāṣir al-Dīn al-Albānī, 2nd edn. (Al-Maktab al-Islāmī wa Dār al-ʿArabiyyah, 1392/1972), p.8.

[6] Ibn Rushd, p.24.

[7] Muḥammad ibn Jarīr al-Ṭabarī, *Tafsīr al-Ṭabarī* (Cairo: Dār al-Maʿārif, n.d.), vol.3, pp. 572–74; and Fakhr al-Dīn al-Rāzī, *Al-Tafsīr al-Kabīr* (Cairo: ʿAbd al-Raḥīm Muḥammad, 1938), vol.5, p.145.

[8] This meaning is demonstrable in verse 2:194: "... whoever then commits aggression against you, commit yet aggression against him accordingly ..."

[9] Muḥammad ibn Aḥmad al-Qurṭubī, *Jāmiʿ Aḥkām al-Qur'an* (Cairo: Maṭbaʿah Dār al-Kutub al-Maṣrīyyah, 1354/1935), vol.2: p.348

[10] Ibid.

[11] According to Islamic jurisprudence, in the absence of other supportive evidence (*qarā'in*), the meaning rendered by the statement of the text (*ʿibārah al-naṣṣ*) prevails over any other meaning extracted by indication (*ishārah*), implication (*dalālah*), or inference (*muqtaḍā*) of the text. The previous explication is therefore obscure and open to question, for it unjustifiably suppresses (*tuʿaṭṭil*) the direct meaning of the verse. See ʿAbd al-Wahhāb Khallāf, *ʿIlm Uṣūl al-Fiqh* (Al-Dār al-Kuwaytiyyah, 1388/1968), pp.143–53;

and ᶜAbd al-Mālik ibn ᶜAbdullah al-Juwaynī, *Al-Burhān fi Uṣūl al-Fiqh*, ed ᶜAbd al-'Aziz al-Dib (Cairo: Dār al-Anṣār, 1400/1979), vol.I, p.551.

12 Al-Ṭabarī, *Tafsīr,* vol.3, p.285.

13 Abū Ḥanīfah, al-Shāfiᶜī, and Mālik distinguish Arab Pagans from non-Arab polytheists, and consider that the verses of *Surat al-Tawbah* are applicable only to the former. See ᶜAlī ibn Muḥammad al-Māwardī, *Al-Aḥkām al-Sulṭāniyyah* (Cairo: Dār al-Fikr, 1404/1983), p.124; Ibn Rushd, p.24; and Muḥammad ibn Idrīs al-Shāfiᶜī, *Al-Risālah,* ed. Ahmad Shākir (n.p., 1309/1891), pp.430–32.

14 Khallāf, p.191.

15 Al-Mundhirī, p.9.

16 Abū Yūsuf, *Kitāb al-Kharāj* (Cairo: Al-Tibā'ah al-Munīriyyah, 1397/1976), p.9.

17 Ibid., p.139.

18 Ibn Rushd, pp.23–24.

19 Such as "fight the 'People of the Book' until they pay *jizyah* ...," or any other statement which is phrased in a way that would include the 'People of the Book' as a whole; i.e., the structure of the sentence would be "fight those who ... " or "fight the 'People of the Book' who ... " rather than "fight those who ... of the 'People of the Book' ..." The article *min* which has been translated as "of" is usually employed, according to Arabic usage, for particularization and separating one group of things or people from another; see al-Juwaynī, vol.1, p.191.

20 Al-Māwardī, p.124.

21 Ibid., pp.125–26.

22 Kamil Salamah al-Daqs, *Al-ᶜIlāqāt al-Dawliyyah fi al-Islām* (Jeddah: Dār al-Shurūq, 1396/1976), p.302.

23 Ibid., p.302.

24 Ibid., citing *Tārīkh al-Ṭabarī*, vol.3, p.236.

25 Al-Daqs, p.303, citing *Futūḥ al-Buldān*, p.166.

26 Al-Daqs, p.308.

27 Ibn Rushd, p.11; Majid Khadduri, *War and Peace in the Law of Islam* (NY: AMS Press,

1400/1979), p.256; and Fatḥī al-Ghayth, *Al-Islām wa al-Ḥabashah ʿAbra al-Tārīkh* (Cairo: Maktabah al-Nahḍah al-Maṣrīyyah, n.d.), p.57, citing *Al-Sīrah al-Ḥalabiyah;* vol.3, p.294.

28 T.W. Arnold, *The Preaching of Islam* (London: Constable and Company, 1332/1913), p.113.

29 Ibid., pp.113–4; Muhammad Haykal, *The Life of Muhammad,* trans. Ismāʿīl al-Fārūqī (North American Trust Publications, 1397/1976), pp.97–101; and Ibn Hishām, *Sīrat ibn Hishām,* in *Mukhtaṣar Sīrah ibn Hishām,* ed. ʿAbdal Salām Hārūn (Beirut: Al-Majmaʿ al-ʿIlmī al-ʿArabī al-Islāmī, n.d.) pp.81–87.

30 The classical definition of *dār al-Islām,* which was formulated by early Muslim jurists, is the territories in which the Islamic law is enforced. See al-Daqs, pp.126-28, Khadduri, *War and Peace,* p.62; and al-Ghunaimi, pp.155–58. Some jurists, such as al-Shawkānī, expand the definition of the territory of Islam to include any area where Muslims can safely reside "even if the territory is not under Muslim rule," quoted in al-Ghunaimi, pp.157-58.

31 Zāhir Riyād, *Al-Islām fi Ethyūbiyā* (Cairo: Dār al-Maʿrifah, 1384/1964), p.46.

32 Ibn al-Athīr, *Al-Kāmil fi al-Tārīkh* (Cairo: Al-Tibāʿah al-Munīriyyah, 1349/1930), vol.2, p.145.

33 Majid Khadduri translated the text of a letter that al-Najāshī allegedly sent to the Prophet. The letter reads: "In the name of Allah, the Merciful, the Compassionate. To Muhammad, the apostle of God, peace be on you. May God shelter thee under His compassion, and give thee blessings in abundance. There is no god but God, who has brought me to Islam. Thy letter I have read. What thou hast said about Jesus is the right belief, for he hath said nothing more than that. I testify my belief in the King of heaven and of earth. Thine advice I have pondered over deeply ... I testify that thou art the apostle of God, and I have sworn this in the presence of Jaʿfar, and have acknowledged Islam before him. I attach myself to the worship of the Lord of the worlds, O Prophet, I send my son as my envoy to the holiness of thy mission. I testify thy words are true." (Quoted in Khadduri, *War and Peace,* pp.205-206).

34 Ibn Hishām, pp.214–15; and Haykal, pp.300–302.

35 Ibn Hishām, pp.256–60; and Haykal, pp.346–54.

36 Ibn Hishām, p.140; and Haykal, p.180.

37 Ibn Hishām, p.142; and Haykal, p.181.

38 Haykal, pp.191-93.

39 Ibid., pp.244–45, and Ibn Hishām, p.175.

40 Haykal, pp.300–301; and Ibn Hishām, p.214.

41 Haykal, p.284; and al-Daqs, p.287.

42 Al-Daqs, p.287.

43 Haykal, p.387.

44 Al-Daqs, pp.287–88, citing Ibn Taymiyyah "Risālah al-Qitāl" in *Majmūʿah al-Rasā'il al -Najdīyah,* pp.126–28.

45 Al-Daqs, pp.128-29.

46 Muhammad Abū Zahrah, *Al-ʿIlāqāt al-Dawlīyyah fi al-Islām* (Cairo: 1384/1964), p.51, quoted in al-Ghunaimi, p.202.

47 Al-Qurṭubī, vol.5, pp.407-12.

48 When incongruence exists between a certain (*qaṭʿī*) and uncertain (*ẓannī*) rule, the certain prevails. Many leading jurists, such as al-Shāfiʿī and ibn Taymiyyah, contend that a Qur'anic verse can only be abrogated by another Qur'anic verse. See al-Shāfiʿī, pp.106–7; and Ṣalāḥ ibn ʿAbd al-ʿAzīz al-Manṣūr, *Uṣūl al-Fiqh wa Ibn Taymiyyah,* (n.p., 1400/1980), vol.1, p.227, and vol.2, p.533.

49 The firm rule (*muḥkam*) is defined by Muslim jurisprudents as a statement whose meaning is clear and unequivocal so that it cannot be considered a subject of *explication de texte* (*ta'wīl*), see Khallāf, p.168.

50 According to Islamic jurisprudence, a firm rule (*muḥkam*) is not the subject of abrogation; see Khallāf, p.168. Al-Ghazālī contends that only the verses that render legal or practical rules pertinent to Islamic law (*ḥukm sharʿī*) are subject to abrogation, while verses which provide general facts (*ḥukm ʿaqli*) are not. See Abū Ḥāmid al-Ghazālī, *Al-Mustaṣfa fi ʿIlm al-Uṣūl* (Cairo: Al-Maṭbaʿah al-Amiriyyah, 1322/1804).

51 Yaḥyā ibn Sharaf al-Dīn al-Nawawī, *Forty Hadith,* trans. Ezzeddin Ibrahim and Denys Johnson-Davies (Beirut: Dār al-Qur'an al-Karīm, 1386/1976), p.59.

52 Al-Māwardī, p.192.

53 Al-Māwardī, p.53.

54 Ibid., p.53.

55 Haykal, p.397, and Ibn Hishām, p.277.

56 Sayyid Qutb, *Milestones* (Cedar Rapids: Unity Publishing Co., n.d.), p.55.

57 Majid Khadduri, *The Islamic Law of Nations: Shaybānī's Siyar* (Baltimore, Md.: John Hopkins University Press, 1386/1966), p.154; and Ibn Rushd, p.22.

58 Referring to women and children as Muslim property does not reflect the pure Islamic perception of human dignity. It should be noted that although Islamic law did not abandon the practice of enslaving prisoners of war, which was a customary law among the Arabs as well as other nations during the time of the Prophet, it did not encourage it either. On the contrary, Islam upgraded the status of the slaves from a mere "property" to persons with certain human rights, and established several avenues through which the slave could be freed, such as *mukātabah* (contracting with one's master for freedom) and *kaffārah* (act of attonement). The Qur'an established two measures for dealing with prisoners of war: they could be either ransomed or freed as a favor and a gesture of goodwill: " ... when you have thoroughly subdued them, then take them as prisoners, and afterward either set them free as a favor or for compensation until the war terminates ..." (47:4). The practice of enslaving the prisoners of war should not be regarded, thus, as a Muslim obligation, but rather as a custom which has been tolerated by the Shariʿah, and could be abandoned by Muslims if deemed harmful to the cause of Islam.

59 Ibn Taymiyyah, *Al-Siyāsah al-Sharʿīyyah* (Dār al-Kātib al-ʿArabī, n.d.), pp.131–32.

60 Qutb, pp.65–67.

61 Haykal, p.303; and Ibn Hishām, p.215.

Selected Bibliography

I. ARABIC

Abū Yūsuf, *Kitāb al-Kharāj.* Cairo: Al-Ṭibaʿah al-Munīriyyah, 1976.

al Daqs, Kāmil Salāmah. *Al-ʿIlāqat al-Dawlīyyah fi al-Islām.* Jeddah: Dār al-Shurūq, 1976.

al-Ghazālī, Abū Ḥāmid. *Al-Mustaṣfa fi ʿIlm al-Uṣūl.* Cairo: Al-Maṭbaʿah al-Amiriyyah, 1904.

al-Ghayth, Fatḥī. *Al-Islām wa al-Ḥabashah ʿAbra al-Tārīkh.* Cairo: Maktabah al-Nahḍah al-Maṣriyyah, n.d.

Ibn al-Athīr. *Al-Kāmil fi al-Tārīkh.* Cairo: Al-Ṭibāʿah al-Munīriyyah, 1349 AH.

Ibn Hishām. *Sirah Ibn Hishām.* In *Tahdhīb Sirah Ibn Hishām,* edited by ʿAbd al-Salām Hārūn. Beirut: Al-Majmaʿ al-ʿArabī al-Islāmī, n.d.

al-Juwaynī, ʿAbd al-Mālik ibn ʿAbdullāh. *Al-Burhān fi Uṣūl al-Fiqh,* edited by ʿAbd al-ʿAziz al-Dīb. Cairo: Dār al-Anṣār, 1980.

Ibn Taymiyyah. *Al-Siyāsah al-Sharʿīyyah.* Dār al-Kātib al-ʿArabī, n.d.

Khallāf, ʿAbd al-Wahhāb. *ʿIlm Uṣūl al-Fiqh.* Al-Dār al-Kuwaytiyyah, 1968.

al-Manṣūr, Sālah ibn ʿAbd al-ʿAziz. *Uṣūl al-Fiqh wa Ibn Taymiyyah.* n.p., 1980.

al-Māwardī, ʿAlī ibn Muḥammad. *Al-Aḥkām al-Sulṭānīyyah.* Cairo: Dār al-Fikr, 1983.

al-Mundhirī, Zakkī al-Dīn, ed. *Mukhtaṣar Ṣaḥīḥ Muslim,* edited by Nāṣir al-Dīn al-Albānī, 2nd edn. Al-Maktab al-Islāmī wa Dār al-ʿArabiyyah, 1972.

al-Qurṭubī, Muḥammad ibn Aḥmad. *Jāmiʿ Aḥkām al-Qur'ān.* Cairo: Maṭbaʿah Dār al-Kutub al-Maṣrīyyah, 1935.

al-Razī, Fakhr al-Dīn. *Al-Tafsīr al-Kabīr.* Cairo: ʿAbd al-Raḥīm Muḥammad, 1938.

Riyād, Zhir. *Al-Islām fi Ethyūbiya.* Cairo: Dār al-Maʿrifah, 1964.

al-Ṭabarī, Muḥammad ibn Jarīr. *Tafsīr al-Ṭabarī*. Cairo: Dār al-Maʿrifah, n.d.

al-Shāfiʿī, Muḥammad ibn Idrīs. *Al-Risālah,* edited by Ahmed Shākir, n.p., 1891.

II. ENGLISH

AbūSulaymān, ʿAbdulHamīd. *The Islamic Theory of International Relations: Directions for Islamic Methodology and Thought*. Herndon, Va.: The International Institute of Islamic Thought, 1987.

Arnold, T.W. *The Preaching of Islam*. London: Constable and Company, 1913.

Haykal, Muhammad H. *The Life of Muhammad,* trans. by Ismāʿīl al-Fārūqī, 8th edn. North American Trust Publications, 1976.

al-Ghunaimi, Muhammad Talaat. *The Muslim Conception of International Law and the Western Approach*. The Hague, Netherlands: Martinus Nijhoff, 1978.

Ibn Rushd, "Chapter on Jihad," in *Bidāyah al-Mujtahid wa Nihāyah al-Muqtaṣid,* trans. by Rudolph Peters in *Jihād in Mediaeval and Modern Islam*. Belgium: E.J. Brill, 1977.

Khadduri, Majid. *War and Peace in the Law of Islam*. New York: AMS Press, 1979.

——*The Islamic Law of Nations: Shaybānī's Siyar*. Baltimore, Md.: Johns Hopkins University Press, 1966.

al-Nawawī, Yaḥyā ibn Sharaf al-Dīn. *Forty Hadith,* trans. by Ezzeddin Ibrahim and Denys Johnson-Davies. Beirut/Damascus: Dār al-Qur'an al-Karīm, 1976.

Qutb, Sayyid. *Milestones*. Cedar Rapids, Ia: Unity Publishing Co., n.d.

Glossary

Abbasid. A dynasty that reigned from the middle of the second century of the Islamic calendar to the eighth century. It dominated particularly the Central Middle East region: Syria, Lebanon, Palestine, Jordan, Egypt, Iraq, Iran, and the Arabian Peninsula.

Abū Ḥanīfa. A jurist of the second century AH and the founder of the first school of fiqh.

Abū ʿUbaydah. A general who led the Muslim armies in the conquest of the Byzantine Empire during the reign of the first Caliph, Abū Bakr.

Abū Yūsuf. A jurist who served as a chief judge during the reign of the third Abbasid Caliph.

Abyssinia. A strong kingdom that flourished in the fourth and sixth centuries AH in North-East Africa, in the region of modern Ethiopia and Eritrea.

Aḥkām. The plural of *Ḥukm*. See *Ḥukm*.

Al-Ṭabarī. A Muslim historian who wrote the first voluminous work describing early Muslim history.

Amān. A permit to enter a Muslim territory *(dār al-Islām),* historically given to a non-Muslim living in a hostile country *(dār al-Ḥarb).*

Banū Qaynuqāʿ. A Jewish tribe that lived in Madinah around the time of the Prophet.

Dār al-Ḥarb. A political community engaged in war and hostilities with the Muslims. The territory of war.

Dār al-Islām. The territories in which Islamic law prevails. The territory of Islam.

Fiqh. A term referring to the various doctrines and rules derived from the Islamic sources by Muslim jurists.

Futūḥ al-Buldān. A voluminous book by the fourth-century AH Muslim historian al-Baladhuri. The book describes in detail the life in various Muslim cities.

Hadith. The written tradition of the Prophet Muhammad.

Hijrah. The literal meaning of the word is emigration. It usually refers to the emigration of early Muslims from Makkah to Madinah. The event marks the beginning of the Islamic calendar.

Ḥudaybiyyah. A place near Makkah where an important peace treaty between the early Muslims and the Quraysh was signed.

Ḥukm. Shariʿah ruling. *Ḥukm* could be a general ruling (*ḥukm ʿām*), or a particular ruling (*ḥukm khāṣṣ*).

ʿIbārah al-Naṣṣ. The direct meaning of a statement.

Jaʿfar ibn Abū Ṭālib. A Companion of the Prophet, who migrated to Abyssinia.

Jizyah. A tax historically imposed on the members of a non-Muslim community.

Khandaq. A trench dug around a city for defense purposes.

Kharāj. A tax imposed on productive land, or herald.

Madinah. A city in West Arabia to the north of Makkah, where the first Islamic community was founded by the Prophet.

Madinan. The adjective for Madinah.

Makkah. A city in West Arabia where the Prophet was born. Makkah is the center that Muslims face during their daily prayers, and the site of the annual pilgrimage (Hajj).

Makkan. The adjective of Makkah.

Mālik. Mālik ibn Anas was a Muslim jurist and the founder of one of the four main schools of fiqh.

Mansūkh. Qur'anic texts that have been abrogated by other texts.

Māwardī. A Muslim jurist who lived in the fourth century AH during the Abbasid Caliphate.

Muḥammad ibn al-Ḥasan. A leading Muslim jurist in the Ḥanafī school of fiqh.

Muḥkam. A firm Shariʿah ruling, which means that a ruling has a clear meaning and no controversial application.

Mushrik. A polytheist who worships idols.

Mu'tah. A town in present-day Jordan, which was the site of the first battle between the Byzantine and Muslim armies.

Najāshī. The king of Abyssinia during the time of the Prophet. He was sympathetic to Muslims and provided protection to Muslims who sought refuge in his kingdom.

Naṣṣ. Literally means "text." It is used often in reference to the Qur'anic text.

Qur'an. The book Muslims believe to be the Word of God revealed to the Prophet Muhammad.

Quraysh. The tribe of the Prophet.

Riddah. The act of renouncing Islam; apostasy.

Salah. Regular prayer.

Salām. Peace.

Sarakhsī. A Muslim jurist of the Ḥanafī school.

Shāfiʿī. A leading Muslim jurist and the founder of the second school of fiqh in the Sunni branch of Islam.

Shām. The region of Syria, Lebanon, Jordan, and Palestine.

Shariʿah. Islamic law.

Siyar. A term used by the Ḥanafī jurists to refer to rulings governing the purpose and method of war.

Sunnah. The tradition of the Prophet.

Surāqah ibn ʿAmr. A member of Quraysh who attempted to capture the Prophet during his journey of emigration from Makkah to Madinah. He later embraced Islam and fought alongside the Muslim armies that conquered Persia.

Surat. A chapter of the Qur'an.

Ta'wīl. A method of interpretation of the Qur'an.

ʿUdwān. Agression.

Ummah. Community of believers, often used to refer to the Muslim community.

Uṣūl al-Fiqh. Islamic jurisprudence.

Zakah. An obligatory charity paid by Muslims. One of the five pillars of Islam.

Index

Other titles by the IIIT in this series

PERSPECTIVES ON ISLAMIC THOUGHT

National Security and Development Strategy
ARSHAD ZAMAN
PB: 969-462-000-7
1990

Nationalism & Internationalism in Liberalism, Marxism and Islam
TAHIR AMIN
PB: 969-462-002-3
1991

Theories of Islamic Law: The Methodology of Ijtihad
IMRAN AHSAN KHAN NYAZEE
PB: 1-56564-081-0
1994

The Socio-Political Thought of Shah Wali Allah
MUHAMMAD AL-GHAZALI
PB: 1-56564-098-5 HB: 1-56564-097-7
2001